Hestia..p 52

Hera..p 54

Demeter..p 58

Aphrodite...p 63

The Children of Theia.......................p 67

Eos..p 67

Selene...p 71

The Children of Themis....................p 74

The Moirai.......................................p 74

The Horae..p 77

The Children of Tethys.....................p 80

Doris..p 84

Amphitrite..p 86

Thetis...p 88

Iris and Arce....................................p 90

The Children of Mnemosyne............p 96

Calliope..p 96

Kleio..p 99

Euterpe..p 100

Terpsichore..p 101

Thalia..p 102

Melpomene...p 103

Erato..p 104

Urania...p 105

Polyhymnia...p 106

The Children of Demeter................p 107

Persephone......................................p 107

The Children of Zeus.......................p 111

Athena..p 115

The Children of Hera and Zeus......p 117

Ate...p 117

Hebe..p 120

Leto..p 121

Artemis..p 125

Artemis and Orion...........................p 126

Asteria...p 130

Arethusa..p 138

Cyrene...p 144

The Children of Aphrodite................p 147

The Three Graces...........................p 148

Calypso...p 156

Circe...p 166

The Sirens.....................................p 169

Pandora..p 172

Psyche..p 175

Gaea and Uranus

Gaea

Gaea is the great mother of all creation, the earth and the heavenly gods. She is the earth. Her husband is Uranus, the god of the sky. She is one of the earliest founding deities called Protogenoi born at the dawn of creation. She has several husbands. The sea gods are her children with Pontus. The Gigantes are her children with Tartaros and all mortal creatures were born directly from her earthy flesh. She is also the mother of Ananke and of the 6 Titanides: who are Theia, Rhea, Themis, Mnemosyne, Tethys and Phoebe and the 6 Titans: Creus, Kronos, Hyperion, Lapetus and Coeus as well as the three Cyclops: Arges, Brontes, Steropes and the Gigantes, the Erinyes (the four furies), Meliae (the Ash Tree Nymphs) and the three 50 headed 100 armed Hekantonkheires: Briareus, Cottus, Gyges.

The 6 Titanides and 6 Titans, children of Gaea.

Ananke

She is the personification of force, necessity, inevitability and compulsion. She is the self-formed primordial creator of the universe along with Chronos, the personification of time. Together in serpent form they tied themselves around the universe crushing the primal egg of creation; the pieces of which became the earth, heaven and the sea to form an ordered universe. She holds a spindle with which she wove creation.

She is the mother of the three fates known as the Moirai and is also mother of Adrasteia, the distributer of rewards and punishments and of Ida. These are the two sisters who raised Zeus in hiding along with the goat Amaltheia. Adrasteia gave the Sphaira, globe of the cosmos to baby Zeus as a play thing.

Ananke

Antheia

Daughter of Melinda, goddess of romantic love and Xenos, god of destruction. Antheia seems to be one of the primordial goddesses who out of the darkness created plant life after Gaea created earth. Antheia became the goddess of gardens and plant growth, flowers and flowery wreathes, swamps, lowlands and marshes, healing, and companionship. Her name comes from the Greek word Anthos which means blossom.

She became an attendant of Aphrodite and a friend of Hera, Iris and Persephone.

Zeus banished her to Crete at the request of her mother who did not approve of her lover Theodric. Crete became her center of worship and her only temple was there.

She spends part of the year with Persephone in the underworld and the rest of the year with Aphrodite.

Antheia has cascading blonde hair by some accounts red and constantly blowing in the wind with a flower crown around her head and her eyes always closed. She has flowers and vines all over her body.

Antheia, goddess of the garden

Theia

Theia is the Titan goddess of light and sight. Daughter of Gaea and Uranus, one of the twelve first generation Titans and Tintanides (titanesses) whom Zeus and the Olympiads overthrew. The Titanides were spared from being cast down into Tartarus as were Cronus, Epimetheus and Menoetius and Prometheus.

She is married to her brother Hyperion. The Titans and Titanides were involved in the creation of mankind and each one gave mankind one of their senses. Hyperion and Theia gave mankind sight.

The ancient Greeks believed that Theia's eyes are beams of light helping mortals to see with their own eyes. She also has the gift of prophecy along with her sisters Phoebe and Themis. She had a shrine in Thessaly.

Theia and Hyperion had three children: Helios, the god of the sun, Selene, the goddess of the moon and Eos, the goddess of the dawn.

Theia, Goddess of Light and Sight

PHOEBE

Phoebe is one of the titanesses, daughter of Gaea and Uranus. With her brother and husband, the titan Coeus she is mother of Leto and grandmother of Apollo and Artemis. Phoebe also is mother of the titans Asteria, the star-goddess and Perses and Pallas. Asteria and Perses had a daughter Hecate, goddess of witchcraft and magic.

Phoebe is the goddess of brightness and radiance and prophecy and oracular intellect like her sister Themis and her mother Gaea. She like all her sisters was never involved in the Titanomachy, war between the Titans and the Olympians and was thus spared from imprisonment down in Tartarus. Instead she took her place at the oracle of Delphi.

She was the third prophetess at the oracle of Delphi after her grandmother Gaea and her sister Themis. However according to Aeschylus, she felt extremely burdened as the prophetess of the oracle and gave the position to her grandson Apollo as a birthday present.

Phoebe

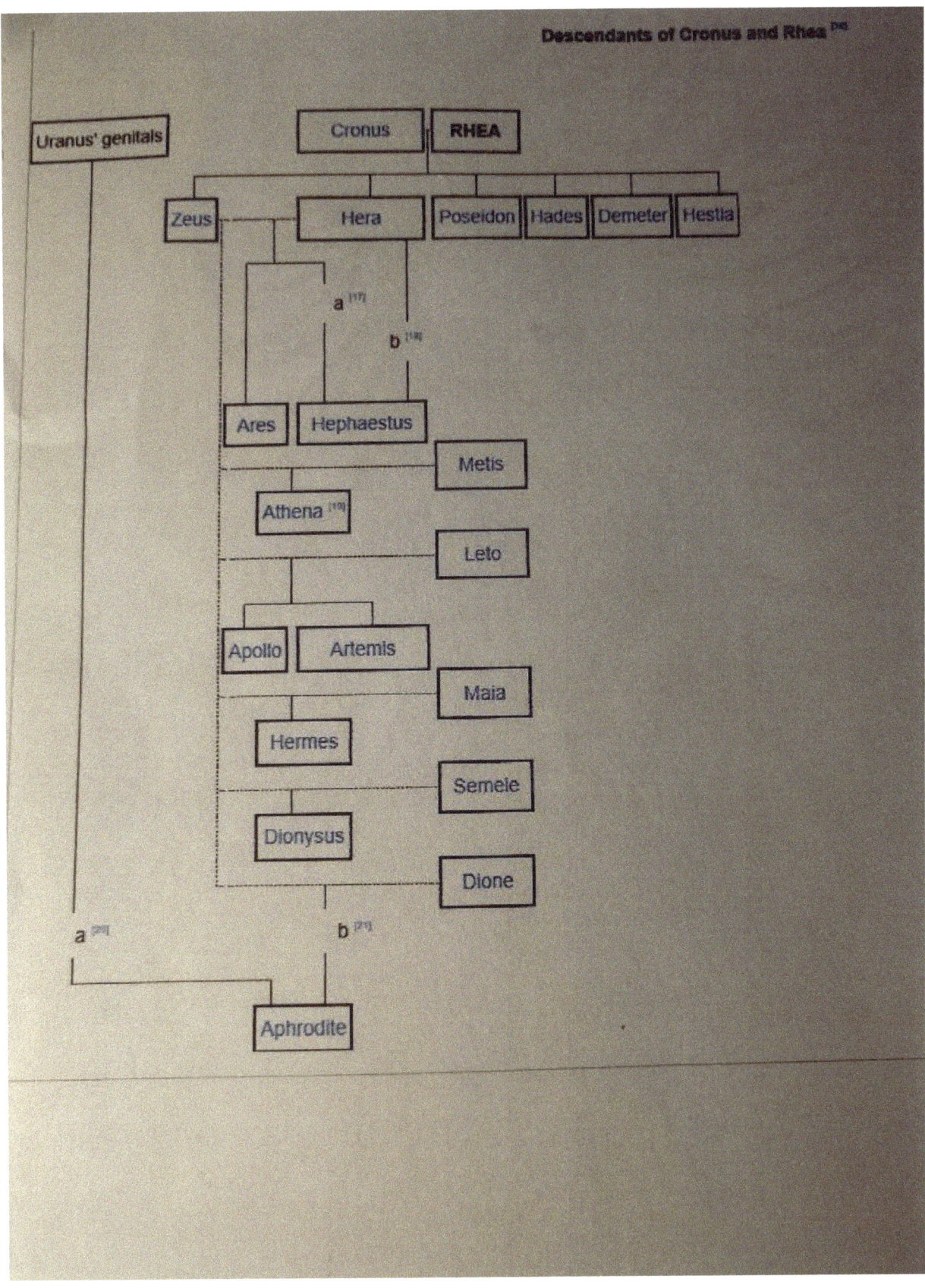

Rhea

Rhea, known to the Romans as Cybele, is daughter of Gaea and Uranus, earth and sky and she is wife and sister of Cronus. She is mother to the Olympian gods but not an Olympian herself. She is the goddess of fertility, motherhood and generation.

Cronus had usurped the throne from his father Uranus. In order to prevent his children from one day doing that to him, he swallowed them as they were born which made Rhea very sad.

She came up with a plan to save Zeus by wrapping a stone in swaddling clothes and feeding it to Cronus. Then she and Gaea hid baby Zeus in a cave on Mount Dikte on Crete where he was guarded by the three Curates and Dactyls (mountain spirits) who did a frenzied dance clacking their swords against their shields to drown out his crying. He was raised by the sister nymphs Adrasteia and Ida daughters of Melisseus and the nanny goat Amaltheia.

This was the beginning of the Titanomachy, the war between the Titans of Mount Othrys and the Olympians led by Zeus over who would rule the universe. Zeus and his Olympians won.

Rhea's other children are Poseidon, god of the sea, Hades, god of the underworld, Hestia, goddess of the hearth, Hera, goddess of nature and marriage and Demeter, goddess of the harvest.

Rhea (Cybele)

Cronus takes over the throne from Uranus as Rhea looks on

Rhea feeding Cronus a stone wrapped in swaddling clothes instead of baby Zeus

Curates and Dactyls drown out the crying of baby Zeus while the nymphs Adrasteia and Ida take care of him in the cave on Mount Dikte on Crete.

Themis

Themis is one of the six Titanides, meaning she is one of the twelve children of Uranus and Gaea. Her sisters are the Titanides: Mnemosyne, Phoebe, Rhea, Tethys and Theia as well as the Meliae (Ash Tree Nymphs) and the Erinyes (the Furies). She is half-sister of Aphrodite.

She is the goddess of good counsel and the personification of divine order, fairness, law, natural law and customs. Her symbol is the scale of balance and her name means divine law or literally "to put in place." She is the organizer of communal affairs of humans especially assemblies. She is a gift from the gods and a mark of civilized existence, right customs, proper procedure, social order and also the will of the gods as revealed by omen.

Her lover is Zeus. Their offspring are the Horae and the Moirai, Astraea and Prometheus. The Erinyes and the Meliae are also her sisters because the gods can have more than one mother and father.

Her ability to foresee the future enabled her to become one of the Oracles of Delphi. She built the Oracle of Delphi according to some while others say she inherited it from Gaea and bequeathed it to Phoebe. This in turn led her to become the goddess of divine justice. She sometimes carries a sword which she uses to cut fact from fiction. When Themis is disregarded, the goddess Nemesis brings just and wrathful retribution. Themis shares the Nemesion temple at Rhamnous.

Themis presides over the proper relation between men and women, the basis of rightly ordered family. Judges are often referred to as "Themistopoloi." She also keeps order on

Mount Olympus. Even Hera calls her "Lady Themis." Themis was present at Delos to witness the birth of Apollo.

Themis, Apollo & Python at Oracle of Delphi. Apollo slays Python.

Tethys

Tethys is one of the Titanides, daughter of Gaea and Uranus, sister of Rhea, Phoebe, Themis, Mnemosyne and Theia. She is the goddess of water, the first spring, the earth encircling, fresh water stream and mother of the Potomai (rivers) the Okeanides (nymphs of springs, streams and fountains and the Nephelais (clouds). Tethys offspring with Oceanus include the river goddesses Metis, Eurynome, Doris, Callirhoe, Clymene, Perse, Idyia, Styx and the other Oceanids

Tethys

Mnemosyne

Mnemosyne is one of the six Titanides, daughters of Uranus, god of heaven and Gaea, goddess of earth.

She is the Titan goddess of memory and remembrance and the inventress of language and words. She represents rote memorization to preserve history and myths before there was writing. It is memory that is the gift that allows us to reason, to predict and anticipate outcomes and is the very foundation of civilization.

When a person dies their soul is given the choice to drink from Lethe, the goddess of forgetting's river where you forget all the pains and terrors of your life and the lessons they taught you or to drink from the Mnemosyne's spring of memory. Those who choose to forget are destined to be reborn to learn the lessons they need and those who choose to remember are admitted to the Elysian Fields to spend eternity in comfort and peace.

She is also a minor oracle goddess presiding over the underground oracle of Trophonius in Boeotia. Initiates go to the oracle temple and are first given water from Lethe to forget their present life and then are given water from Mnemosyne to drink to remember all they are about to learn from the oracle. They are then placed in seclusion for several days in the tomb of Trophonius, the earth god undergoing a mock burial alive to await the arrival of the oracle. If the initiate is found worthy the oracle explains the mysteries of life to them while in trance in the afterlife. When the initiate returns to the realm of the living, the priests place them on the Throne of

Mnemosyne and they tell all they remember and have learned while in the other world.

Mnemosyne also presides at the temple of Asclepius, the god of healing to help the ill remember any visions they have while in trance in the Asclepeion temple.

Mnemosyne reigns over the hills of Eleuther in Pieria near Mount Olympus. Zeus came there and stayed with her 9 days and after a year she gave birth to the 9 muses:

Calliope, (beautiful voice), the muse of eloquence and epic poetry, Kleio, the muse of history, Erato, the muse of love poetry, Euterpe, the muse of music, Melpomene, the muse of tradegy, Polyhymnia, the muse of sacred music, poetry and hymns, Terpsicore, the muse of dance, Thalia, the muse of comedy and Urania, the muse of Astronomy.

Mnemosyne; restoring memory of a soul

The Enrinyes

The Erinyes, the four furies are daughters of Gaea although they may also be the daughters of Nyx, another Protogenoi from creation time who is the goddess of the night. Some people think they are the daughters of Hades and Persephone.

The Erinyes are also known as the goddesses of vengeance who haunt humans who lie under oath. Three of them are Megaera (jealous rage), Alecto (endless) and Tisiphone (vengeful destruction). The fourth Telphousia is also the wrathful aspect of Demeter, the goddess of the harvest.

The task of the Erinyes is to hear complaints of mortals against youth who are insolent to their elders, hosts who are rude to guests, householders or city councils who are unfair to tenants or their citizens. It then becomes the task of the Erinyes to hound the culprits relentlessly.

Later in this book we will talk about the Trojan War but the most famous story about the Erinyes involves Orestes. He was the son of King Agamemnon of Mycenae and of Clytemnestra. When Agamemnon returned from the Trojan War he was killed by his wife's boyfriend Aegisthus who had moved in with her while he was away. Orestes when he became an adult avenged his father by killing his mother and her lover with the help of his sister Elektra. According to the play by Aeschylus, The Erinyes haunted Orestes and he took refuge with Apollo in his temple who lulled two of them into sleep. Clytemnestra's ghost tried in vain to awaken them. Apollo purified Orestes with pig's blood and in the end he is forgiven his crime and the Erinyes turn into the Eumenides (Kindly).

Orestes and the Erinyes (the Four Furies)

Nyx

Nyx is the goddess of the night and a protogenoi. Her parent was Khaos (air). Her siblings are Erebus, Gaea and Tartarus. She is also the mother of Hypnos (sleep) and Thanatos (death). With her husband Erebus (darkness) who was also her brother, they had the children Aither (light) and Hemera (day). Gods and goddesses could marry their brothers and sisters and some like Nyx have only one parent while others like the Moriea have more than two parents.

Nyx, a primogenoi, goddess of the night

Second Generation of Titans: The children of Rhea and Cronus:

Rhea and Cronus had six children. They are Hestia, Demeter, Hera, Hades, Poseidon and Zeus. Cronus had swallowed the first five to prevent one of them from taking over his throne but clever Rhea fed him a stone wrapped in swaddling clothes instead of Zeus and had Zeus raised in secret in a cave on Mount Ida in Crete.

Eventually Zeus grew up and married his first wife, Metis who is the Titaness daughter of the Titans Oceanus and Tethys. Zeus wanted to liberate his siblings from Cronus's belly. So Metis tricked Cronus into swallowing a potion of herbs that she told him would make him invincible but instead he vomited up Zeus's 5

siblings fully grown. Then with Zeus as their leader, the Titanomachy, war between the Titans and the Olympians (Zeus and his siblings) began. The Olympians won and they banished their father to Italy. (Not such a bad gig.)

Zeus liberates his siblings from Cronus's belly with the help of Metis's potion.

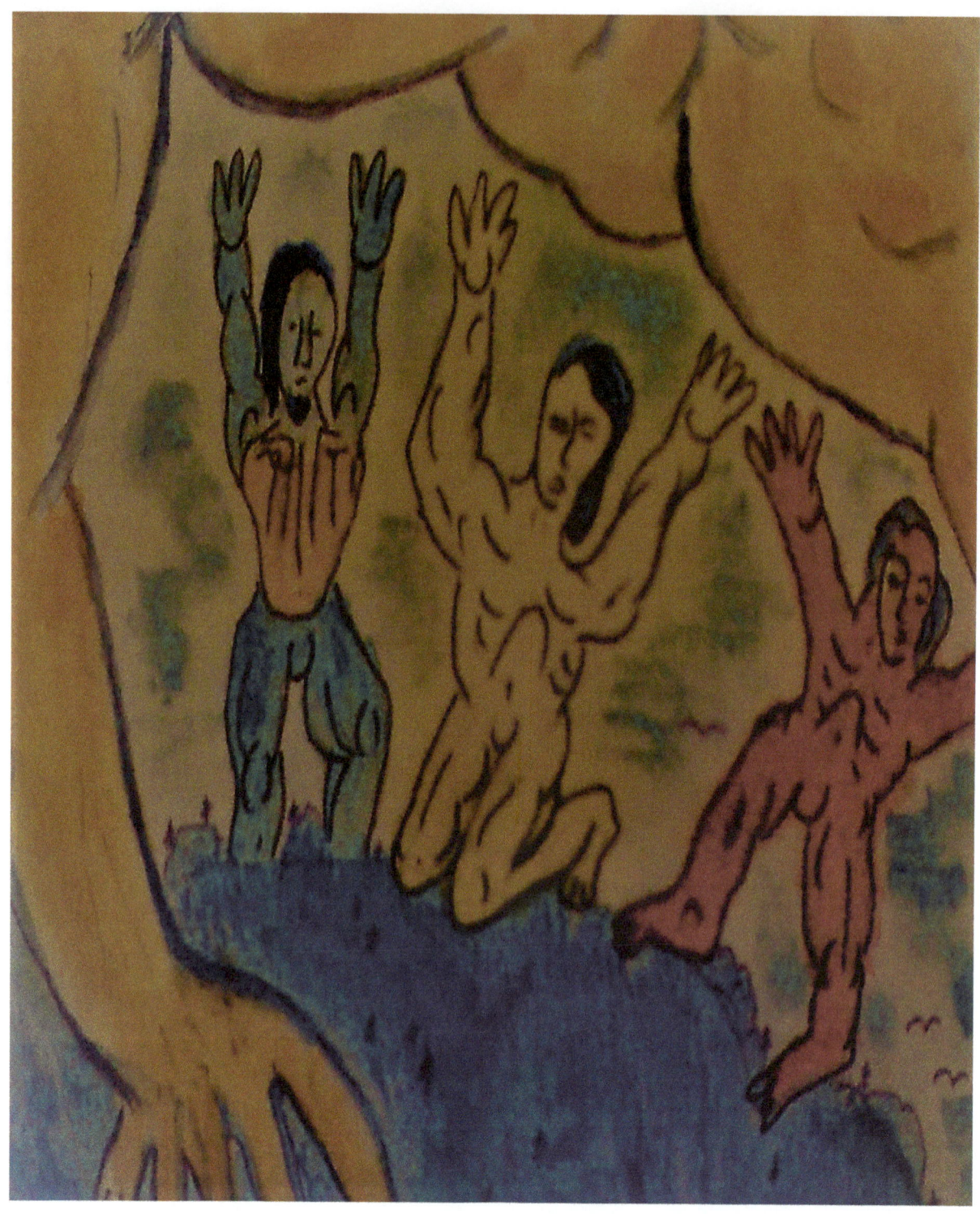

Zeus, Poseidan and Hades banish Cronus to Italy

Hestia

Hestia is the eldest of Rhea's three daughters. Her sisters are Hera and Demeter. She is the goddess of the family and civic hearth, architecture, correct order in family, home and state.

Although Apollo and Poseidon both courted her, she told Zeus she did not wish to marry or ever have a lover in return for which Zeus gave her the honor of presiding over all sacrifices at every hearth in every household.

She gave up her seat on Mount Olympus to tend the fire of Mount Olympus and to let Dionysus take her place. Besides she didn't want to be involved in the quarrels of the twelve Olympian gods and goddesses.

She was central to daily worship in Greek and Roman homes.

Apollo and Poseidon court Hestia under Zeus's gaze.

Hera

The next eldest daughter of Rhea is Hera.

Hera is the Queen of Nature, the Queen of the gods and goddesses. She is also the goddess and protectress of women, marriage and childbirth. She is daughter of Cronus and Rhea.

The cow, the lion and the peacock are considered sacred to her.

Hera was born on the island of Samos.

The greatest and earliest free-standing temple to Hera is the Heraion of Samos which still stands, although in ruins, on the isle of Samos today in the plain between Pithagorion and Ireon.

After Zeus swallowed Metis to prevent his children growing up to overthrow him, Zeus needed a new wife. Zeus tricked Hera into marrying him. He wanted his sister Hera but she refused him. Thus, began his career of clever shape shifting. He disguised himself as a cuckoo bird caught in the rain which tapped gently on the window begging for shelter. She took the bird in and dried it off and told it she loved it at which point Zeus turned back into himself and said:" OK, now you have to marry me." She became his principle wife and queen of heaven.

Hera persuaded Aphrodite to make Medea fall in love with Jason because he needed her help to nab the Golden Fleece away from her father Aeetes, King of Colchis. However, Hera decided to help Jason because she hated his rival Peleus. Hera spends most of her time jealously tormenting her unfaithful husband Zeus's lovers and his half mortal son Herakles.

Greek Goddesses for Girls   by Brian H Appleton

Demeter

Demeter, daughter of Cronus and Rhea is the goddess of the harvest, grain, agriculture, growth and nourishment, giver of food and the fertility of the earth. She also presides over sacred law in a civilized agricultural society and over the cycle of life and death. She and her daughter Persephone by Zeus were central figures of the Eleusian Mysteries before the Olympians came along.

The most famous story about Demeter involves the kidnapping of her daughter Persphone which we will go into later in this book.

Demeter lives on Mount Olympus. Her symbols are the cornucopia, wheat, a torch and bread. She had five lovers one after another starting with Iasion, Zeus, Oceanus, Karmanor, Poseidon and Triptolemus. She had eight children: Persephone, Despoina, Arion, Plutus (blind god of wealth), Pjilomelus, Eubuleus, Chrysothemis and Amphitheus I.

Her festival was the Thesmophoria which was held in honor of her and Persphone and was the most widespread festival in ancient Greece held as far away as Eritrea and Sicily. It was held annually in Autumn at the time of planting seeds and of harvest and celebrated human and agricultural fertility.

Only adult women were allowed in the festival and the rites practiced during the festival were kept secret. The festival dates back to 1100 BC pre-Ionion Greece. It was restricted to citizens and married women and may have been limited to the aristocracy. Although in Athens the festival lasted only three days in Sicily they carried on for ten days.

Another less famous story about Demeter involves Erysichthon, son of Triopas, King of Thessaly. Erysichthon ordered all the trees in the sacred grove of Demeter to be cut down for a great hall he wanted to build. One huge oak was covered with votive wreaths for every prayer Demeter had granted and so Erysichthon's men refused to cut it down. Grabbing an axe he cut it down himself, killing the dryad nymph within. Her dying words were a curse on him. Demeter carried out the curse by talking Limos, the spirit of unrelenting and insatiable hunger into Erysichthon's stomach. The more he ate, the hungrier he became. He ran out of things to sell in exchange for food so he sold his own daughter Mestra into slavery for the food money. Poseidon who had been her former boyfriend freed her and gave her the gift of shape shifting. Her father sold her over and over and

she would shape shift to escape but no amount of food could satisfy his hunger so finally he ate himself. End of story.

Demeter, Goddess of the harvest

Aphrodite

Aphrodite is the goddess of love and beauty. Her parentage is not clear. Some say she was born from the sea foam after Cronos Spay his father Uranus and his wee wee fell into the sea. Others say her parents were Zeus and Dione.

Her symbols are myrtle, roses, doves, sparrows, swans, pearls, the mirror and sea shells. She is associated with the planet Venus. Her Roman name is Venus.

Her first husband is Hephaestus, god of metallurgy, son of Zeus. But she had many lovers including the Gods: Ares, Poseidon, Hermes, Dionysus and the mortals: Adonis and Anchises.

She also has many children, the most famous of whom is Eros who is called Cupid by the

Romans. We will talk about her other famous children later.

Legend has it that the Tyrrhenic Venus lost her pearl necklace when she emerged from bathing in the sea. It broke into tiny splinters and this is how the seven islands of the Tuscan Archipelago have originated of Elba, Capraia, Pianosa, Giglio, Gorgona, Montecristo and Giannutri.

Aphrodite's main temples are the Aphrodite Pandemos on the southwest slope of the Acropolis in Athens and in Corinth on the Acrocorinth, which was one of the main centers of her cult.

In Sparta she was worshipped as Aphrodite Areia which means warlike because of her relationship with Ares.

Her main festival was called the Aphrodisia which was celebrated all through Greece and especially in Athens and Corinth on the fourth day of the month of Hekatombaion in honor of her role in the unification of Attica.

Very ancient statues of Aphrodite have been found in Cythera, Sicily and Corinth.

Tyrrhenic Venus and the origins of the Tuscan Archipeligo.

The children of Theia:

Theia had three children by the titan Hyperion. They were Eos (the dawn), Helios (the sun) and Selene (the moon)

Eos

Eos, the goddess of the dawn was married to her cousin Astreus, the god of the dusk but then she had an affair with Ares, the Olympian war god. This made Aphrodite, his sister jealous. She put a curse on Eos giving her a never-ending desire for handsome young men.

She kidnapped Cephalus, Tithonos, Orion and Cleitus. She gave immortality to Cleitus. When she asked Zeus to give immortality to Tithonos, she forgot to ask Zeus to also give him perpetual youth. As he aged for eternity he shriveled and shriveled becoming ever smaller until one day he turned into a grasshopper.

By Tithonos before he became a grasshopper she bore two sons: Memnon, who became the King of Ethiopia and Emathion who became the king of Arabia.

Greek Goddesses for Girls   by Brian H Appleton

Eos and Tithonos

Selene

Selene is the Titan goddess of the moon. She is the daughter of Helios and Theia. She drives every night across the skies in her silver moon chariot drawn by two snow-white horses as opposed to the golden sun chariot drawn by four.

Apollonius of Rhodes is one of the many poets who tell how Selene, the Titan goddess of the moon, loved a mortal named Endymion. According to Apollonius, Selene believed Endymion to be so beautiful that she asked Zeus, to grant him eternal youth so that he would never leave her.

Alternatively, Selene so loved how Endymion looked when he was asleep in the cave on Mount Latmus, near Miletus in Caria that she entreated Zeus that he might remain that way. In either case, Zeus granted her wish and put him into an eternal sleep. Every night, Selene visits him where he sleeps to gaze upon his beauty. Somehow Selene and Endymion had fifty daughters who are equated by some scholars with the fifty months of the Olympiad.

Yet a third version of this story says that Endymion was a handsome shepherd-prince whom Zeus offered his choice of destinies. He chose immortality and youth in eternal sleep. He was laid out in a cave on Mount Latmus where Selene visits him each night. Selene is linked to Artemis as well as Hecate; all three are considered lunar goddesses.

Selene and Endymion

The Children of Themis:

The Moirai

The three fates, the Moirai are the daughters of Zeus and Themis and half-sisters of the Horae.

They sit nearest to the throne of Zeus on Mount Olympus and weave with shuttles of Adamant and give him counsel.

Some say their mother was Nyx, the goddess of the night. Perhaps deities can have more than one mother. They are also the children of Ananke.

The three fates are named Clotho, Lachesis and Atropos. Clotho spins the thread of life from her distaff onto her spindle. Her Roman equivalent is Nona (the Ninth) who is called upon in the ninth month of pregnancy.

Lachesis (meaning "alloter" or drawer of lots) measures the thread of life allotted to each person with her measuring rod. Her Roman equivalent is Decima (the tenth.)

Atropos (meaning "inexorable", "inevitable", "unturning") is also sometimes called Aisa. She is the cutter of people's life thread with her abhorred shears. Her Roman equivalent is Morta ("Dead One").

According to Plato, the three Moirai sing in unison with the music of the Sirens. Lachesis sings the things that were. Clotho the things that are and Atropos the things that are to be.

Pindar in his Hymn to the Fates honors them and calls them to send their sisters the Horae, Eunomia (lawfulness), Dike (Right) and Eirene (Peace) to stop internal civil strife.

The Moirai: Clotho, Lachesis and Atropos

The Horae

The hours are the goddesses of the seasons spring, summer and fall. There are six half-sisters all together. The children of Zeus and Aphrodite are the seasons: Spring, Thallo; the bringer of blossoms and protector of young people; Auxo; the increaser of plants and Carpo; the bringer of food linked to autumn and harvest. Carpo is the main guardian of the path to Mount Olympus, concealing it in the clouds.

The children of Zeus and Themis are the goddesses of order and justice as well as guardians of the gates to Mount Olympus. They are: Dike, goddess of moral justice; Eunomia, goddess of order and governing according to good laws and Eirene, goddess of

peace and wealth who carries a cornucopia, scepter and torch.

The Horae Thalo, Auxo and Carpo

The Horae Dike, Eunomia and Eirene with baby Plutus, god of wealth

The Children of Tethys

Tethys offspring with Oceanus are the river goddesses Metis, Eurynome, Doris, Callirhoe, Clymene, Perse, Idyia, Styx and the other Oceanids.

Metis

Metis is the daughter of Titans Oceanus and Tethys. She is the goddess of good counsel, advise, planning, cunning, craftiness and wisdom. She advised Zeus during the Titan War and devised the plan which forced Cronus to regurgitate his children.

Metis prophesied that she would give birth first to a girl and then to a boy who was destined to rule the world by fate. Zeus in fear of the prophecy that Metis would bear him a son more powerful than himself swallowed the pregnant Metis whole. Their daughter Athena Nike was later born full grown from Zeus head liberated by her half-brother Hephaestus when Zeus asked him to relieve him of his tremendous head ache and Hephaestus obliged by striking his head with an axe.

When Athena was born, Metis had a chance to escape from Zeus's stomach through the same hole in his head but she was exhausted from the labor of child birth and also she was still in love with Zeus even though he had been unfaithful to her so she opted to stay inside him and became part of him and continued to give him wise counsel from within.

Metis inside Zeus

Doris

The name Doris (Δωρίς) means bounty. She is an Oceanid, a sea nymph whose name represents the bounty of the sea. She is the daughter of Oceanus and Tethys and the wife of Nereus. She is also aunt to Atlas, the titan who was made to carry the sky upon his shoulders, whose mother Clymene is a sister of Doris. Doris is mother to Nerites and the fifty Nereids, including Thetis, who is the mother of Achilles, and Amphitrite, Poseidon's wife, and mother of Triton.

Doris is considered the fertility of the ocean, goddess of the rich fishing-grounds found at the mouths of rivers where fresh water mingles with the brine. Being an Okeanide meant she is a sister of the Rivers. Her name is connected with two words: Dôron meaning "gift" or "abundance," and Zôros meaning the "pure" and "unmixed." Zôros is often used to describe fresh water or the pure soul of a woman, and from this derived words such as zôrua "the transference of running water" and zôrux "water conduit."

Doris and a hippokampoi

Amphitrite

Amphitrite is the daughter of Doris and Nereus, eldest of her 50 Nereid sisters and wife of Zeus's brother Poseidon god of the sea. Amphitrite is the queen of the sea—the loud moaning mother of fish, seals and dolphins. She rides in a chariot drawn by sea horses called hippokampoi and wears her hair in a net with a pair of crab claws for horns.

Amphitrite

Thetis

Thetis is the goddess of water, daughter of Doris and Nereus and granddaughter of the Titaness Tethys. Thetis is the leader of the Nereids. Her marriage to the hero Peleus was the cause of the Trojan War

Thetis saved Zeus from a plot to overthrow him by Hera, Poseidon and Athena when she summoned Briareus, the hundred-armed monster to Olympus to protect him.

She and the Oceanid Eurynome also caught Hephaestus when he was cast out of Mount Olympus and took care of him on the Island of Lemnos where he smithed making armor for them.

Both Zeus and his brother Poseidon courted Thetis. However, Themis, the oracle had prophesied that if Zeus married Thetis, their child would over throw him so Zeus had her married off to the mortal hero Peleus. At first, she rejected Peleus. On the advice of the ancient sea god Proteus, Peleus caught her when she was asleep and bound her tightly to keep her from shape shifting but she did shift anyway though he held on to her. She became water, fire, a raging lion and still he held onto her so she finally agreed to marry him.

The wedding of Thetis and Peleus was celebrated on Mount Pelion, outside the cave of Chiron, the centaur, and attended by the deities: there they celebrated the marriage with feasting. Apollo played the lyre and the Muses sang. At the wedding Chiron gave Peleus an ashen spear that had been polished by Athena and had a blade forged by Hephaestus. While the Olympian goddesses brought him gifts: from Aphrodite, a bowl with an embossed Eros, from Hera a chlamys while from Athena a flute. His father-in-law Nereus endowed him a basket of the salt called 'divine', which causes overeating, good appetite and good digestion. Zeus then bestowed the wings of Arce to the newly-wed couple which were later given by Thetis to her son, Achilles for his feet.

Iris and Arce

Arce and Iris are sister Titanides, daughters of Thaumas and Elektra. They both had wings and are associated with rainbows. Iris is the primary rainbow and Arce the secondary one next to it. During the Titanomachy war between the Olympiads and the Titans, the two sisters found themselves on opposite sides. Iris was messenger of the Olympiads and Arce was messenger of the Titans. So after the Titans lost, Zeus took her wings and tossed Arce into Tartarus along with the other titans.

Iris and Arce

At the wedding of Thetis and Peleus, the god of the sea, Poseidon gave Peleus the immortal horses, Balius and Xanthus. Eris, the goddess of discord, had not been invited, however. She threw, in spite, a golden apple into the midst of the goddesses that was to be awarded only "to the fairest." It was Paris who determined who was the fairest which eventually led to the Trojan War.

Thetis by Peleus, gave birth to their child Achilles, whom she saved after he was wounded in the heel during the war by snatching him away to the island of Leuke in the Black Sea where he transcended death.

Thetis and Peleus

BIA

Bia is the daughter of the 2nd generation of Titans Pallas and Styx. Bia's grandmother is Tethys. Bia is the goddess of strength, the personification of force, power, might, bodily strength and compulsion. Her siblings are brother Kratos(strength), sisters Nike (victory) and Zelos(rivalry.) They sided with Zeus during the Titanomachy (Titan War) and became his winged enforcers in attendance at his throne on Mount Olympus. When Prometheus angered Zeus by giving mankind fire he ordered Bia and Kratos to arrest Prometheus and he ordered his son Hephaestus, god of metallugy to put him in chains and chain him to the Caucasus Mountains where an eagle ate his liver daily and it grew back nightly for eternity until years later Herakles saved him by slaying the eagle who was Zeus's symbol.

Kratos, Hephaestus, Prometheus and Bia

The Children of Mnemosyne

Mnemosyne's lover is Zeus. He came and spent 9 days with her and after that she gave birth to the 9 muses. Their eldest daughter is Calliope.

Calliope, the muse of eloquence and epic poetry

She is chief muse. Her name means beautiful voice, ecstatic harmony and she presides over eloquence and epic poetry.

She is considered the wisest of the muses, as well as the most assertive. She is said to have been the lover of Ares and bore him four sons, Mygdon, Edonus, Biston and Odomantus who became the founders of the Thracian tribes. Although they may have been the children of her namesake Calliope, daughter of the river god Nestus.

Calliope also had two famous sons Orpheus and Linus. Their father was either Apollo or Oeagrus, King of Thrace.

She is said to have defeated the daughters of Pierus, King of Thessaly, who had challenged her to a singing competition and then as punishment for their presumptuousness, she turned them into magpies.

Some believe she is the mother of the Sirens. She is believed to have been Homer's muse for the Illiad and the Odyssey.

Calliope and the daughters of King Pierus

Kleio

Next daughter is Kleio, the muse of history.

Euterpe, the muse of music

Terpsichore, the muse of dance

Thalia, the muse of comedy

Melpomene, muse of tragedy

Erato, the muse of erotic poetry

Urania, muse of astronomy

Polyhymnia, muse of sacred hymns & poetry

The Children of Demeter

Demeter's children are Melinoe, Zagreus and Persephone.

Persephone

Persephone is the goddess of spring. The story goes that Hades fell in love with Persephone and kidnapped her to his underworld. Demeter went looking all over for her with the help of Hecate, daughter of Perses and Asteria. Perses is son of the Titans Crius and Eurybia and Asteria is daughter of the Titans Phoebe and Koios. Hecate is the goddess of way finding, witchcraft and magic. Hecate has three heads and is known as the torchbearer.

Finally, Demeter found Persephone with the help of Arethusa, a Nereid, daughter of Nereus who in the form of an underground spring saw Persephone in the underworld as the unhappy queen of Hades. Also Demeter learned that Zeus who was her husband and Persphone's father had helped Hades, his brother kidnap her because Hades was madly in love with her. Demeter in anger then refused to let the earth bear fruit until her daughter was returned to her. Zeus and Hades gave in and let Persephone return home but since she had eaten some of Hades food, a few pomegranate seeds while captive, Zeus said she had to spend part of the year with Hades. Thus, the seasons. Winter when Demeter misses her daughter Persephone while she is with Hades and spring when she returns to the surface and is reunited with her mother Demeter.

Persephone, with Hades in hot pursuit

Demeter and Hecate searching for Persephone in a cave

The Children of Zeus

Zeus swallowed his first wife Metis to avoid having a child who would take over his throne as he had done to Cronus. What he did not realize at the time was that Metis was pregnant with Athena. Years later one day he developed a bad headache...a killer headache so he asked his son Hephaestus by his second wife and sister Hera, to help relieve him of his headache. Hephaestus was the god of metallurgy. He was lame and homely and husband of Aphrodite. So he picked up an axe and split open Zeus's head which didn't kill him of course because he is a god but it did relieve him of his headache and out popped Athena Nike, the goddess of just wars fully grown and armored.

Zeus swallowing his first wife Metis.

Birth of Athena Nike from Zeus's head

So after Athena was born from Zeus's head, Metis was too tired from labor to escape herself and besides despite Zeus's transgressions, she still loved him so she stayed inside his stomach and his head and since she is the goddess of deep thought and wise counsel, she became part of his mind and gives him guidance.

ATHENA

Athena in her non-combative form is the goddess of wisdom, handicraft and patroness of Athens. In fact she is called Athena Pallas and is the patroness of all city states. Her symbol is the owl as well as olive trees, snakes and the Gorgoneion, a protective amulet with the likeness of Gorgon's head on it. In her Athena Nike combative form, she wears a helmet and carries a spear and she is known for her strategic skill in warfare and is the companion of heroes and patroness of heroic endeavors. She aided the heroes Perseus, Herakles, Bellerophon and Jason.

She had no husband and no children of her own but adopted Erichthonius of Athens.

She watched over her half-brother Herakles who although a hero got into big trouble when he was drunk. The 12 labors of Herakles were to atone for his sins committed while he was drunk including killing his own first wife Megara and children.

Here is Athena knocking out drunken Herakles with the flat of her sword to keep him out of trouble.

The Children of Hera and Zeus

Hera and Zeus's children were Angelos, goddess of the underworld, Ares, god of war, Eileithyia, goddess of childbirth, Enyo, goddess of war and destruction, Eris, goddess of strife and discord, Hebe, cup bearer to the gods and Hephaestus, god of metallurgy.

Hebe is also the fourth and last wife of Herakles.

ATE

Another daughter of Zeus according to Homer or of Eris according to Hesiod is Ate. She is the goddess of mischief. She leads both men and gods to acts of rashness and inconsiderate actions and to suffering.

She tricked Zeus upon the birth of Herakles into taking an oath which the jealous Hera

(Herakles mother was the beautiful mortal woman Alcmene) used to transfer Zeus's power to Eurystheus that was meant for Herakles. Zeus upon discovering his rashness, tosses Ate off Mount Olympus banishing her to earth to make trouble for mankind and later to avenge evil deeds and inflict just punishments on offenders, similar to Nemesis and the Erinyes.

Zeus tossing Ate out of Olympus

Hebe, the cupbearer of the Olympians riding on her father Zeus's back in his eagle form.

Leto

Leto is a daughter of the Titans Coeus and Phoebe, the sister of Asteria. She was born on the island of Kos.

She is an early and favorite lover of Zeus but while she was pregnant by him, he tricked his sister Hera into marrying him. Remember the gods are not bound by our rules. Hera was extremely jealous of Leto and created problems for her and pushed her out of Olympus.

Poor Leto wandered the earth because no one would let her stay in their home for fear of Hera. As if that were not bad enough Hera had the dragon Python chase her. Zeus saved her by sending Boreas, the North Wind to carry her off to sea. She finally landed on the rocky and barren island of Delos which had nothing to lose so they accepted her. The other goddesses came to help her with her childbirth except for jealous Hera who detained Eileithyia, the goddess of childbirth but Iris eventually succeeded in bringing her to the island. Leto first gave birth to Artemis and after another nine days of labor to Apollo.

Still trying to escape Hera's wrath she fled to the island of Lycia. The peasants there prevented her from drinking from their well so she turned them into frogs.

Both her fast-growing children became powerful archers who protected her. When Apollo was only four days old he slew Python and then when the Euboen giant Tityus tried to ravage Leto, her two children slew him.

They wished to avenge their mother and protect her honor so when Niobe bragged that she bore Zeus seven sons and daughters Artemis and Apollo slew all but one of them.

This impressed Zeus. She regained his favor so he lightened her punishment after their son Apollo killed the Cyclops. Leto then spent most of her time hunting with Artemis.

She sided with the Trojans during the Trojan War and helped Aeneas heal from his wounds.

Leto with her twins Apollo and Artemis

Artemis

Artemis is the twin sister of Apollo. She is the goddess of the wilderness and forests, animals, the hunt, the moon and protector of young girls as well as curing disease in women. She also is a goddess associated with childbirth. The deer and the cypress are sacred to her. She was widely worshipped throughout ancient Greece and her priestesses were virgins. In Roman times she was called Diana.

Just like Athena and Hestia she asked her father Zeus to keep her single and chaste. She is a virgin and never married nor had a lover.

Both Artemis and Apollo carry bows and arrows and are very protective of their mother Leto.

Artemis is very protective of her own virginity. When the poor hunter Acteon accidently came upon her naked bathing in a stream in the forest she turned him into a stag and he was killed by his own hounds. When Siproites was just a young boy, he also accidently saw her unclothed so she turned him into a girl.

In her youth Artemis bravely approached Hephaestus and the Cyclops on the Island of Lipara and asked them to make her a bow and arrow. She went to Pan, the god of the forest and he gave her six female dogs and six male dogs which she used to capture six golden horned deer which she used to pull her chariot.

Artemis and Orion

Artemis did have a long-time hunting companion in the mortal Orion. They also had foot races and enjoyed athletics together. Orion was said to be the handsomest man on earth and was well loved by mortals and gods for his great friendship and company. Artemis and Orion became close friends and that was the closest she had to a love interest. But one day her brother Apollo mistook their friendship and thought they were falling in love and in order to protect her chastity as well as to feed the jealousy he was feeling he sent a giant scorpion to kill Orion. Orion fought it valiantly but could not defeat it so finally as the scorpion had backed him up to the sea, he decided to try to outswim it. When he was just a speck on the horizon, Apollo lied to Artemis and told her that it was an evil man named Candaon who had just ravaged one of her virgin priestesses named Opos. She took up her bow and arrow and let fly an arrow at the speck of Orion and inadvertently killed her best friend. She found Opos and seeing that she was unharmed soon figured out what Apollo had done. She retrieved Orion's body and Asclepius tried to revive it with Gorgon blood to no avail. Artemis killed the scorpion and took Orion's body and put it in the stars as the constellation Orion which we can see to this day as a tribute to her friend and a reminder that men and women can enjoy many kinds of friendship. She took the body of the slain scorpion and placed it behind Orion in the heavens as a reminder of the treachery of those who are false to their lovers and themselves.

Artemis with her boyfriend Orion in foot race

Asteria

Asteria is the daughter of Titans Phoebe and Coeus. Asteria and her brother Perses had a daughter Hecate, goddess of witchcraft and magic.

Asteria is the goddess of shooting stars and of prophetic dreams and astrology. She is very beautiful like her sister Leto and so caught the eye of Zeus who pursued her. She turned herself into a quail to escape him and leaped into sea to become the island of Asteria later changing its name to Delos where her sister Leto gave birth to Artemis and Apollo

Asteria evades Zeus by turning into a quail and then diving into the sea to become the island of Delos

Children of Zeus continued...

Maia

Maia, is the eldest of the Pleiades, the daughters of Atlas and Peione. She is a very shy goddess and lives in a cave by herself in the mountains of Cylene trying to avoid entanglements with the gods. One night Zeus came to her and then she bore him a son, Hermes, the messenger of the gods. The baby Hermes the same night of his birth crawled away during the night while she slept, growing so quickly into an adult that he stole some of Apollo's cattle and also invented the Lyre with a tortoise shell. Apollo complained to Zeus and eventually Hermes traded his Lyre for the cattle he had stolen and the lyre became Apollo's symbol and musical instrument of choice from then on. Maia also adopted and raised Arcas, the son of Zeus and Callisto because when his wife Hera discovered their affair in a rage she turned Callisto into a bear. Callisto and Arcas eventually became the stellar constellations Ursa Majore and Minore.

Maia, titan goddess of Spring

Semele

Semele is a demi-goddess, daughter of the Boetian hero Cadmus and Harmonia (daughter of Ares and Aphrodite.) She bore Zeus a son, Dionysus, the god of wine, grape harvest, ritual madness, religious ecstasy and theater.

There are different stories about Semele but one version says she was serving as a priestess of Zeus. One day after she slaughtered a bull at his alter, she swam in the river Asopus to wash off the bull's blood. Zeus in his guise as an eagle flying over the scene fell in love with her. They met secretly on many occasions. When she became pregnant with Dionysus, Hera discovered their affair. Hera disguised herself as an old woman and befriended Semele. Semele eventually confided in the old lady that she was having a secret affair with Zeus. Hera in disguise, pretended not to believe her and planted a seed of doubt in Semele's mind about whether her lover was actually Zeus. So next visit Semele asked Zeus if he would grant her a wish. He agreed and then she asked him to reveal himself in all his glory as Zeus. He begged her not to ask him to do that. He tried to reveal the weakest thunder bolts he could come up with. Mortals cannot look at gods without burning up so even though she was only half mortal she disintegrated. Zeus managed to grab the embryo Dionysus and sew him into his thigh and a few months later he was born from Zeus's thigh. This is where Dionysus picked up the nick name of "Twice Born."

Later when Dionysus grew up, he went and rescued his mother from Hades and she became a goddess on Mount Olympus with a new name Thyone and she presided over his Dionysiaque festivals.

Semele and Zeus

Arethusa

Arethusa is a Nereid, daughter of Nereus and a nymph of a sacred spring on the Sicilian Island of Ortygia. One day the beautiful Arethusa came across a clear stream and was bathing in it not realizing it was the river god Alpheus who of course fell in love with her. After discovering his presence, she fled as she wished to remain a chaste attendant of Artemis but Alpheus pursued her. After a long chase she prayed to Artemis for protection and Artemis hid her in a cloud but she began sweating profusely from fear and turned into a stream. Artemis broke the ground giving Arethusa another chance to flee. She traveled under the earth to the island of Ortygia but Alpheus also flowed through the sea to the island of Ortygia and mingled with her waters.

Arethusa and Alpheus and Artemis

Panacea

Panacea is the goddess of universal remedy. She is the daughter of Asclepius, demi-god and hero, son of Apollo and the mortal woman Koronis of Thessaly. Asclepius is the god of medicine and patron of the Asklepiades, the ancient guild of doctors. His father Apollo and the centaur Chiron taught him the art of healing.

Some accounts say he was abandoned as a baby by his mother in shame for his illegitimacy near Epidaurus and raised by a dog and a goat. Other accounts by Pindar and Ovid say that Apollo had Koronis killed by Artemis for cheating on him with a lover named Ischys.

At any rate, with Epione, goddess of soothing pain, Asclepius had five daughters: Hygieia (goddess of health and hygiene), Iaso (goddess of recuperation from illness), Aceso (goddess of the healing process), Aglaea (goddess of the glow of good health) and Panacea (goddess of universal remedy) and two sons Podaleirius and Machaon. These two sons were legendary healers in their own right and war heroes in the Trojan War. They led 30 ships for Thessaly and were two of the soldiers inside the Trojan Horse.

The European Rat Snake or Elaphe Longissima in Latin also known as the Asclepius Snake is one of the tools for healing used by Asclepius and his daughter Panacea. The Rod of Asclepius has this snake entwined around it not to be confused with the Caduceus of Hermes which has two of these snakes entwined around his staff.

The ancient Greek playwright, Aristophanes wrote a play called "Plutus" in which the Goddess Panacea tries to cure him of his

blindness. It was a comedy. Plutus is the god of wealth who is blind because people become rich whether they are good or bad or deserve it or not. Somethings never change no matter how many millennia pass by.

Panacea tries to cure Plutus of his blindness as her father Asclepius looks on and her sisters arrive in the background.

Cyrene

According to Pindar, Cyrene is the daughter of Hypseus, King of the Lapiths. Others think she is the daughter of the river god Peneus and is a nymph not a mortal. With Apollo she mothered Aristaeus and Idmon, while with Ares she mothered Diomedes of Thrace.

The story goes that she was a fierce huntress second only to Artemis at the hunt. One day while she was watching over her father's cattle and sheep, a lion attacked them. She wrestled him down with her bare hands. Remember in Greco-Roman times there were Eurasian lions that were actually twice the size of African lions. This is why you always see Herakles and later Alexander The Great wearing lion capes.

It so happened that Apollo was watching her take down the lion and immediately fell in love with her and carried her off to Libya to found the city of Cyrene in the region of Cyrenica both named after her.

Other stories say that Apollo transformed Cyrene into a nymph to give her longer life.

Cyrene wrestling the lion while Apollo watches unbeknownst to her

The Children of Aphrodite

Aphrodite had 21 children. With Ares she had Eros (love), Phobos (fear), Deismos (dread), Harmonia(harmony), Adestia(revenge) Pothos (desire), Anteros (requited love) and Himeros (lust).

With Hermes: Hermaphroditus.

With Poseidon: Rhodos and Eryx.

With Dionysus: Peitho, The Graces and Priapus.

With the mortal Anchises: Aneas.

With the mortal Adonis: Golgos and Beroe

With the mortal Butes: Eryx and Meligounis.

Adopted son: Phaeton, whose parents were Eos and Tithonos.

The Three Graces or Three Charities

Daughters of Aphrodite and Dionysus are AGLAIA, EUPHROSYNE and THALIA. Aglaia personifies elegance. Euphrosyne personifies mirth and Thalia personifies youth and beauty or brightness, joyfulness and bloom.

Some believe they are the daughters of Zeus and Hera or Eurynome, daughter of Oceanus or of Helios and Aegle, daughter of Zeus. We aren't sure or maybe they had more than two parents.

The three graces, Aglaia, Euphrosyne & Thalia

Anchises

Anchises and his son Aneas were Trojans. Aneas married Creusa, daughter of King Priam and their son was Ascanius. Paris was Aneas's brother in law. It is no wonder then that Paris favored Aphrodite since she was an in law, in the beauty contest that Eris, the goddess of chaos, strife and discord, daughter of Zeus and Hera created between Hera, Athena and Aphrodite by tossing her apple of discord into their midst at the wedding of Thetis and Peleus to which she was not invited with a note "for the most beautiful." The beauty contest came to be known as the Judgement of Paris.

It is responsible for starting the Trojan War because as a reward for choosing Aphrodite, she told Paris he could have any mortal woman he desired for his wife. He chose Helen and kidnapped her away from Sparta to Troy. The problem was she was already married to Meneleus, King of Sparta. So Meneleus and his brother Agamemnon, prince of Mycenae and the hero Achilles (son of Thetis and the mortal Peleus) and Odysseus, King of Ithaca and others formed a league with their armies united to go to Troy to get Helen back. Thus, began the Trojan War which lasted ten years. Homer wrote about this in his famous Illiad.

In the end when the Trojans lost, Aneas and his father Anchises and his son Ascanius escaped to Latium though Creusa died during the escape. So you see Ascanio is quite an ancient name. The Aeneid by the Roman Virgil, is the story of their travels from Troy to Latium.

It is believed by some that the Trojans who escaped to Italy became the Etruscans. The

Etruscan alphabet, a syllabary is called Linear B and is Asiatic in origin.

Judgement of Paris. Eris lurks upper right.

After the Trojan War poor old Odysseus, King of Ithaca and his men got lost and were captured by the Cyclops and imprisoned in his cave. Odysseus devised a plan which succeeded in poking out the Cyclops's eye with a burning log from his hearth fire when he fell asleep and then he and his men escaped back to their ship by tying themselves to the underside of the Cyclops's giant sheep so he could not feel them anywhere as the sheep went out to pasture.

As a consequence of Odysseus (Ulysses in Latin) blinding the Cyclops, he pissed off his father Poseidon, who made rough seas and sent his ship off course to the sirens, to the monsters Scylla and Charybdis and to the goddess Calypso and the goddess Circe among other misadventures which caused him to take ten years to get back home to his wife Penelope who faithfully waited for him

despite endless attempts by other men to marry her. This story is all told in Homer's Odyssey and the Trojan War in Homer's Illiad.

Calypso

Most people believe Calypso is the daughter of the Titan Atlas and Pleione although Hesiod said she is the Oceanid daughter of Tethys and Oceanus. Calypso is a goddess nymph who lives on the island of Ogygia. Her symbol is the dolphin. According to Homer's Odyssey, Calypso detained Odysseus on the island of Ogygia for seven years, offering him immortality in exchange for marrying her.

Calypso enchants Odysseus with wine and with song as she weaves on her golden loom.

But eventually Odysseus cannot bear being separated from his wife Penelope any longer and prays to his patron goddess Athena for help. She asks Zeus to order Calypso to release him which she eventually does reluctantly. By some accounts Calypso bore Odysseus a son named Latinus although most people think that Latinus was his child by Circe. By other accounts Calypso bore him two sons, Nausithous and Nausinous.

Regarding Calypso's father, Atlas he was condemned by Zeus to hold up Gaea, the earth for eternity after losing the Titanomachy rather than being cast into Tartarus with the other Titans who lost the war against the Olympians. Atlas was the son of the Titan Lapetus and the Oceanid Asia or Clymene. He had many children besides Calypso, mostly daughters including the Hesperides, the Hyades and the Pleiades.

Calypso holding homesick Odysseus hostage

Medea

Another child of the second generation Titan Helios, the god of the sun by Perse was their son Aeetes, King of Colchis. Aeetes married Idyia, a daughter of Oceanus and Tethys, and she bore him a daughter named Medea who had magical powers and the gift of prophecy. She is the niece of Circe.

Hera asked Aphrodite and Hecate to cast a spell on Medea to make her fall in love with Jason so she would help him get the Golden Fleece away from her father, King Aeetes. The reason she helped Jason was she wanted to get revenge against King Peleus.

Peleus was the son of Tyro who was the son of Salmoneus whose second wife was named Sidero meaning the iron one. When Peleus grew up he murdered his father Tyro's step mother Sidero because she had so mistreated his father Tyro while he was growing up. The problem was that Sidero sought refuge from Peleus and his twin brother Neleus's pursuit by hiding in Hera's temple which Peleus then entered and murdered her on the alter to Hera which was a sacrilege.

The Golden Fleece of the winged ram, was the symbol of kingship and authority and Jason was ordered by King Peleus to recover it from King Aeetes of Colchis so he could place him on his rightful throne of Iolcus in Thessaly.

King Aeetes in Colchis gave Jason three tasks he would need to accomplish before he would relinquish the Golden Fleece to him. One was to plow a field with a team of fire breathing oxen which he had to capture and hitch to yokes. Medea gave him a fire proof salve to rub on. The second was to sow a field with dragons' teeth which immediately sprouted into soldiers who were to attack Jason but forewarned by Medea, he threw a rock into their midst and thinking one of them had thrown it they all fought and killed each other. Finally King Aeetes assigned him the task of killing the sleepless dragon which guarded the Golden Fleece. Medea put the dragon to sleep with narcotic herbs. Then Jason took the fleece and sailed away with Medea whom he had promised to marry. To distract her father from pursuing them she killed her brother Absyrtus and cut him into pieces and scattered his parts on an island her father went to recover instead of pursuing them.

On the way home they stopped in Crete where they were challenged by Talos, the giant bronze robot man who guarded Crete. He had one nail which held him together. Medea hypnotized him with drugs and told him that if he removed the nail she would make him immortal which he did and then bled to death.

When Jason returned with the fleece to Iolcus, King Peleus still refused to relinquish the throne to him. Medea tricked King Peleus's daughters by showing them that she could make an old ram young again by cutting it into pieces and boiling it in special herbs. Which when she demonstrated, a young ram jumped out of the pot. So the daughters cut their father into pieces and threw him into the pot and that was the end of King Peleus.

Medea and Jason then fled to Corinth. In Corinth, Jason abandoned Medea and their children for Glauce, the daughter of the King of Corinth. Medea took her revenge by sending a dress and a golden coronet covered in poison as a present to Glauce which resulted in the death of Princess Glauce and her father the King. Medea continued her revenge by murdering her own children by Jason and then she flew to Athens in a chariot driven by dragons given to her by her grandfather Helios, the sun god. Before she arrived in Athens, she stopped in Thebes and undid a curse that Hera had placed upon Herakles that had led to his killing his best friend Iphitus. But the Thebans threw her out despite Herakles protests and she went on to Athens where she met and married King Aegeus. They had one son Medus but their marital bliss was shattered when Aegeus's long-lost son Theseus showed up.

Determined to protect her son Medus's inheritance of the throne she tried to convince Aegeus that Theseus was not his son and a usurper to his throne. Just as she handed Theseus a cup of poison, Aegeus recognized his sword as the one he had given him in childhood to use when he came of age. Aegeus knocked the cup out of Theseus's hand and Medea and Medus fled back to Colchis to discover that her father Aeetes had been dethroned by his brother Perses. So she killed her uncle and restored her father to the throne. This is her story according to the playwright Euripides. But according to the historian Herodotus Medea and Medus fled from Athens in her flying chariot and landed in the Iranian plateau and they lived among the Aryans, who changed their name to Medes in her honor. The Medes were the Kurds.

At any rate there are many versions and endings for the story of Medea which was already quite an old story by the time it appeared in Hesiod's Theogony around 700 BC so we may never know which story is true and anyway it's all Hera's fault for putting a spell on her to start with.

Medea

Circe

Circe is the goddess of magic and sorcery. She is thought to be the daughter of the Titan Helios and Perse, one of the 3000 Nereids. Her brothers were Perses and Aeetes, keeper of the Golden Fleece and her sister Pasiphae was married to King Minos and mother of the Minotaur.

With the use of magic potions and her wand she transformed her enemies into wild beasts.

Some say that she was exhiled to the solitary island of Aeaea by her father Helios for killing her husband the prince of Colchis. Then she left or destroyed the island and moved to Italy to Capo Circeo.

It is on the island of Aeaea that she entertained Odysseus's men and then drugged them and turned them into pigs. Odysseus goes to rescue them and encounters the god

Hermes (son of Zeus and Maia, the eldest of the Pleiades, daughters of Atlas and Pleione) disguised as a man who gives him an herb called moly to protect him from Circe. He overpowers Circe and forces her to transform the pigs back into his men. Odysseus soon became Circe's lover and he and his men lived with her in luxury for a year before his men finally persuade him to continue his journey home in search of Ithaca.

Hermes approaches Odysseus while Circe turns his men into pigs

The Sirens

The sirens are the daughters of the river god Achelous while their mother is uncertain; either the muse Terpsichore or Melpomene or Calliope or the Pleiade Sterope. Euripides, in his play Helen, called them daughters of Chthon (Earth). The Greeks said they have wings while the Romans associated them more closely with the sea. There are many stories about sirens in ancient Greece and various authors give them different numbers and different names some say there are three. Hesiod said they are named Thelxinoe, Peisinoe and Ligeia.

They lure sailors to their deaths by shipwreck on the rocky coast of their island by enchanting them with their song. There is disagreement on which island they live on. It may be Sirenum, Scopuli or Anthemusa or

Cape Pelorum or on Sirenuse near Paestum or on Capri.

In Homer's Odyssey there were two sirens whom he did not name. Odysseus was curious about what the sirens would sing to him, so on the advice of Circe, he plugged his sailors ears with bees wax and had them tie him tightly to the mast and ordered them to leave him tied up no matter how he begged to be set free.

This is what the sirens sang to him:

"Come this way, honored Odysseus, great glory of the Achaians, and stay your ship, so that you can listen here to our singing; for no one else has ever sailed past this place in his black ship until he has listened to the honey-sweet voice that issues from our lips; then goes on, well-pleased, knowing more than ever he did; for we know everything that the Argives and Trojans did and suffered in wide

Troy through the gods' despite. Over all the generous earth we know everything that happens."

Odysseus and the Sirens Thelxinoe, Peisinoe and Ligeia

Pandora

After Prometheus betrayed the Olympians by giving mortals fire, Zeus was determined to counteract his blessing so he commissioned his son Hephaestus, the metallurgist to fashion a woman out of earth. All the gods were so taken by her beauty that they bestowed upon her all their best gifts.

Pandora was the first mortal woman. According to Hesiod, Zeus then presented Pandora to Prometheus's brother Epimetheus to take for his wife. She opened a jar left in his care which contained sickness, death and many other evils to plague mankind. Although she closed the lid as fast as she could, the only thing left in the jar by then was hope.

Others say the jar was full of blessings which would have been preserved for the human race had they not been lost by Pandora opening the jar out of curiosity. There is also dispute over whether it was a jar or a box.

The creation of Pandora, first mortal woman

Psyche

Psyche is the goddess of the soul. Her parents were an unknown mortal king and queen. In ancient Greece she was portrayed as a butterfly. Her husband is Aphrodite's son Eros. Their daughter is Hedone.

Here is the story of Psyche:

She started out as a beautiful princess who was so very beautiful that people came from far away to see her. People believed she was the next Aphrodite and began to worship Psyche abandoning the temples of Aphrodite, the true goddess of beauty.

When Aphrodite learned her temples had been left barren because people had gone to worship some princess she desired revenge and called on her son Eros, the seducer to help her exact revenge. She told Eros to make Psyche fall in love with the most wretched, impoverished man in the world with no social status, security or inheritance.

Instead Eros fell in love with Psyche himself the instant he saw her or some say he inadvertently pricked himself with one of his arrows. At any rate Eros decided to disobey his mother's orders.

Meanwhile men continued making the pilgrimage to view Psyche to see her beauty but none sought her hand in marriage although marriages were arranged for Psyche's two less beautiful sisters.

Psyche's father not knowing what to do sought advice from the Oracle of Delphi who made him sad by telling him to dress her all up as a bride and set her on the top of a high mountain as it was her destiny not to marry a mortal but rather to marry a fierce barbaric snake monster with wings who brought pain to every moving creature he encountered with torch and dart who even Zeus and the other gods feared and even the rivers and Hades dark realm of the dead shuddered at the sight of him.

Despite her parents' grief and the sorrow of others in their kingdom, Psyche fearlessly went to the mountain top and stepped off, to be rescued by the Zephyros, the god of the West wind of spring, who carried her gently to a golden palace where she was bathed and fed by invisible servants. That night her newly found husband Eros came and made love to her but as day broke he was not there. He remained invisible during the day while becoming visible only at night making love to her in the dark so she could not see him. Soon Psyche became pregnant.

Despite all their wealth, Psyche became lonely spending most of her time alone, so she begged her husband to bring her sisters to her. Despite his warning that they would cause her downfall, he consented.

All this time Psyche's sisters had been endlessly searching for her. They were quite surprised when Zephyros showed up and carried them to a golden palace where their lost sister was waiting for them.

Their happiness soon turned to jealousy when they saw their sister's riches and they concluded that her husband was a god although Psyche herself did not know that yet. After they had bathed, eaten a sumptuous meal and caught up on gossip including asking Psyche who her husband was (which Psyche avoided answering because she didn't know), Psyche filled her sisters' arms with treasures and called for Zephyros to carry them home.

Upon their return to the mountain top, her sisters complained to each other about how horrible their own marriages were and how unfair it was that while they were treated no better than maidservants in their own homes, their younger sister lived a life of luxury. They complained that she had been arrogant rushing them away with tiny presents which were nothing compared to her wealth and how she had called upon Zephyros to take them home as though she were a goddess. The two jealous sisters decided that they would think up a way to punish her for her arrogance.

Not long after that, Psyche wanted to see her sisters again, even though Eros told her that they were setting traps for her and trying to get her to reveal the identity of her husband (which Psyche herself still did not know as she had never seen him). Eros also informed Psyche that they would soon be starting a family and that she was already pregnant and that if Psyche disclosed his identity that the child would be mortal but if she kept it secret it would be a deity.

Eventually however Eros consented and allowed Psyche to bring her sisters to visit. Once again they pressured her to reveal who her husband was. This time Psyche made up a tale that he was a middle age businessman which contradicted her original tale. The fact that Psyche did not know who her husband really was, confirmed their suspicions that he was a god.

Shortly after, her wicked sisters visited again. This time they told Psyche that they had heard from the Oracle that her husband was in fact a venomous serpent who was fattening her up and when she grew to full term pregnancy, it would eat her and the child she carried inside her. They advised her to hide a lamp and dagger so that she might see for herself and if it were true then Psyche should kill the serpent. Despite her better judgement she did as her sisters advised.

As night fell Zephyros took her sisters back to the mountain and Psyche went to bed where she was soon joined by her husband. She waited until she heard the soft breathing of his sleep and then got out her lamp and knife. She saw Eros and his bow, arrows and torch. Psyche pricked herself with one of Eros's arrows and fell deeply in love with her husband. Psyche bent over and kissed the sleeping god repeatedly. Psyche accidentally dripped some hot oil from her lamp on Eros' shoulder burning him badly. He woke up and saw his wife above him holding a knife and instantly flew away. Psyche grabbed hold of her husband and held on as tightly as she could for as long as she could eventually falling off and landing in a field at which point Eros continued his flight to his mother to get healed.

Psyche searched and searched for her lost husband eventually coming to the kingdom where one of her sisters lived. Upon arrival there she realized what her sisters had done. Psyche then told her sister that her husband had been none other than Eros and that when he had seen her with the dagger he had dismissed her claiming he would marry her sister instead. Upon hearing these words Psyche's sister went to the mountain top despite the harsh wind and leapt off thinking Zephyros would come for her but instead she crashed on the peaks below and her body was ripped to shreds.

Shortly after, Psyche came to the land where her other sister lived and told the same story. Her sister similarly leapt off the mountain where she shared the same fate.

After the deaths of her sisters, Psyche began roaming the lands in search of her husband who had arrived at his mother's palace for medical treatment. A Seagull arrived at the Ocean and found Aphrodite and told her that her son had been gravely wounded. Upon hearing this she asked who had hurt her beardless boy? When told it was the mortal woman named Psyche her anger about Eros's wound disappeared and she became enraged with him instead and threatened to take away his bow & arrow as well as his torch.

Aphrodite set off searching for Psyche and met Demeter and Hera along the way who tried to persuade Aphrodite not to pursue her. The two were hoping this might make Eros happy.

Psyche spent her time still wandering the Earth looking for her husband. She prayed to all the gods but her prayers fell on deaf ears. Eventually she came to a temple belonging to Demeter. Psyche begged for her help but the goddess of the grain turned her down not wishing to anger Aphrodite.

Psyche left the temple and eventually arrived at yet another temple. This one belonging to Hera. Psyche asked for help saying that she knew Hera was the goddess of pregnant women. Hera however gave the same answer as Demeter further explaining that Aphrodite was searching for Psyche and the law says no goddess may give sanctuary to a servant (who Aphrodite saw Psyche as) whose master is seeking him or her.

When she heard that Aphrodite was looking for her, Psyche pondered whether she should surrender herself to Aphrodite in an attempt to minimize the goddess' rage.

Aphrodite who had been unable to locate Psyche went to Hermes and told him to make it known that no man or god should give Psyche shelter. Aphrodite also promised a reward of seven sweet kisses to whoever brought Psyche to her. When she heard of the reward Aphrodite was offering, Psyche made up her mind and went to the palace of the goddess.

Upon arriving at Aphrodite's palace, Psyche was whipped and burned before being brought into the presence of the goddess of beauty who upon seeing Psyche's pregnant state mocked her and beat her and then told Psyche the only way she could earn her husband back was through laborious tasks she would assign her.

Aphrodite took Psyche to a granary where she mixed the smallest seeds into a heap and commanded her to separate them by type. Aphrodite then set out for a wedding. Psyche stared unmovingly at the pile frozen in shock. Miraculously however a number of ants appeared. Their leader asked his ants to take pity on her and to help her because she was refined and Eros's wife. A small army of ants arrived and separated the seeds. By the time Aphrodite returned the task was complete. Rather than being pleased Aphrodite angrily told her that it didn't count because the ants had done the work for her. Aphrodite then threw the girl some moldy hard black bread and left her to sleep on the cold stone floor while the goddess herself went to sleep on a comfortable couch.

As dawn arrived Aphrodite pointed to a flock of golden sheep. Aphrodite told Psyche to retrieve some of the wool to make a shirt with. When she approached she saw how violent the rams were and that they had poisonous breath. Psyche lost hope and decided to drown herself in the waters of a nearby stream. As she approached, the reeds spoke to her and told her that while fighting now, if she waited they would grow tired and fall asleep. The reeds told her further that once they were asleep she could freely go and take wool that had gotten tangled on branches. Psyche heeded their advice and waited for the rams to tire themselves out from fighting each other and then she walked over and plucked the wool off the brambles and returned them to her mistress who rather than being pleased was upset that Psyche had survived. The next day Aphrodite took Psyche to the foot of a mountain and pointed at its peak, and told her that way up at the top of a dizzily high cliff was the source of a dark spring that cascades down into the neighboring valley whose marshes feed the River Styx (the river of hatred) and feed the hoarse streams of the River Cocytus (the river of lamentation). Aphrodite asked her to hurry and bring back in a small jug she had given her, some icy water drawn from the stream's highest point, where it gushes out of the cliff. As Psyche climbed she soon discovered how slippery the rocks were and she was also challenged by snakes. Once again with hope gone, Psyche decided to throw herself off the mountain peak. But before she could jump, the Eagle of Zeus swooped down with the vial and filled it with water from that infernal spring. Upon returning successfully, Aphrodite accused her of being a witch.

She passed the first three tests, but the fourth was harder. Psyche had to go down to Hades and obtain some of Persephone's beauty, because Aphrodite's beauty had diminished from the stress of caring for her wounded son, Eros. Psyche descended to Hades, fed a cake to Cerberus, the three-headed dog guardian at hell mouth and paid Karonte, the boatman of the dead, to ferry her across the Akheron River. Next, she asked Persephone for some of her beauty. Persephone accepted and gave it to her in a box. During her return, Psyche decided to take this beauty for herself but, when she opened the box, a Styx dream possessed her. Eros flew quickly to her and deleted the dream from Psyche's mind. Then, Eros asked permission from Aphrodite and Zeus to marry Psyche and they accepted. Aphrodite danced at the wedding and Psyche and Eros had a daughter called Hedone and Psyche was made a goddess.

Psyche and Eros

The End

Index

Absyrtus……………………………………p 156

Aceso………………………………………..p 136

Achaians……………………………………p 165

Achilles……………………………………p 81, 82, 87, 146

Acropolis…………………………………p 64

Acrocorinth………………………………p64

Acteon……………………………………p 120

Agamemnon……………………………..p 44

Aglaea………………………………………p 136

Aglaia……………………………………..p 143

Adestia……………………………………p 142

Adonis……………………………………p 64

Adrasteia…………………………………p 15, 28, 32

Aeaea………………………………………p 161

Aeetes……………………………………p 56, 154, 161

Aegeus..p 158

Aegle..p 143

Aegisthus..p 44

Aeneas..p 118

Aeneid...p 146

Aeschylus.................................... p 4, 24, 44

Aither...p 46

Akheron..p 184

Alcmene...p 113

Alecto..p 42

Alexander the Great......................p 139

Alpheus...p 133, 134

Amaltheia......................................p 15, 28

Amphitheus I.....................................p 59

Amphitrite..p 80

Ananke.........................p 8, 13, 15, 16, 71

Anchises..p 145

Angelos..p 112

Anteros..p 142

Antheia..p 17

Anthemusa......................................p 164

Aphrodisia......................................p 64

Aphrodite.......................................p 18, 33, 64, 86, 106

Aphrodite Areia............................p 64

Apollo...p 44, 53, 86, 92, 117

Apollonius of Rhodes....................p 71

Arabia...p 68

Arcas...p 128

Arce...p 87

Arges...p 13

Argives..p 165

Ares...p 64, 91, 112

Arethusa...p 102, 133, 134

Arion..p 59

Aristaeus...p 139

Aristophanes..................................p 4, 136

Artemis...p 23, 117, 119, 120

Aryans...p 159

Ascanius...p 145

Asclepius...p 41, 122, 135, 138

Asklepiades......................................p 135

Asclepeion..p 40

Asopus..p 130

Asteria...p 23, 102, 116, 130

Asia...p 152

Astraea...p 33

Astronomy.......................................p 40, 100

Ate..p 112, 113, 114

Athena..p 78, 79, 85, 106

Athena Nike....................................p 77

Athens...p 60, 65, 66, 110, 157

Atlas...p 80, 127, 151, 162

Attica..p 65

Atropos..p 71, 72, 73

Auxo...p 73

Balius...p 170

Bia..p 89

Bellerophon..................................p 110

Beroe...p 142

Biston..p 91

Black Sea....................................p 87

Boeotia.......................................p 39

Boreas..p 116

Briareus......................................p 87

Brontes.......................................p 13

Butes..p 142

Cadmus......................................p 130

Caduceus....................................p 136

Calliope......................................p 40, 91, 93, 164

Callirhoe.....................................p 36, 76

Callisto.......................................p 127. 128

Calypso......................................p 13, 149, 151, 156

Capo Circeo................................p 166

Capraia.......................................p 64

Capri..p 165

Carpo...p 73, 74

Cephalus……………………………………..p 67

Charybdis……………………………………..p 149

Chiron……………………………………….p 85. 135

Chlamys……………………………………..p 85

Chronos………………………………………..p 15

Chrysothemis………………………………..p 59

Circes…………………………………………p 149

Cleitus………………………………………p 67

Clotho ………………………………………p 70, 71, 72

Clymene……………………………………p 36, 76, 80, 152

Clytemnestra……………………………….p 43

Cocytus……………………………………..p 183

Coeus………………………………………..p 13

Colchis……………………………………p 55, 154, 158, 161

Corinth……………………………………p 64, 65, 157

Cottus………………………………………..p 13

Crete………………………………………p 17, 26, 31, 47, 156

Creusa……………………………………..p 145, 146

Crius………………………………………..p 102

Cronus..p 20

Curates...p 26, 31

Cybele..p 26, 28

Cyclops..p 13, 121, 138, 149

Cylene..p 127

Cyrene...p 139, 140, 141

Cyrenica..p 140

Cythera..p 65

Dactyls...p 26, 31

Deismos...p 142

Delos..p 24, 116, 125

Delphi..p 23, 33, 35, 171

Demeter..p 27, 47, 58, 102

Despoina...p 59

Diana...p 120

Dike..p 71, 73, 75

Diomedes...p 1400

Dione...p 63

Dionysus...p 52, 63, 131

Doris..p 36, 80, 82, 84

Edonus...p 91

Eileithyia..p 112

Eirene...p 71, 73, 75

Elba..p 64

Elektra..p 43, 86

Eleusian Mysteries..........................p 58

Eleuther..p 40

Elysian Fields.................................p 39

Eos..p 21, 67, 69, 142,

Emathion...p 68

Enyo..p 112

Epidaurus..p 135

Epimetheus......................................p 20, 167

Erato..p 40, 99

Erebus..p 45

Erinyes..p 13, 32, 42, 44, 113

Eris..p 6, 86, 112, 145, 148

Eritrea...p 59

Etruscans..p 146

Eros...p 63,85, 142, 170,181

Erysichthon...p 60

Eryx...p 142

Ethiopia...p 68

Euboen..p 117

Eubuleus..p 59

Eumenides...p 43

Eunomia..p 71, 73, 75

Euripedes..p 41, 64, 159

Euterpe...p 40, 95

Eurynome..p 36, 76, 84, 143

Gaea..p 6, 13, 23, 36, 152

Giannutri...p 64

Gigantes..p 13

Giglio..p 64

Glauce...p 157

Golden Fleece..p 55,154,156, 161

Golgos...p 142

Gorgon……………………………………………p 110

Gorgona…………………………………………..p 64

Gorgoneion……………………………………..p 110

Gyges……………………………………………..p 13

Hades……………………………………………..p 27, 42, 103, 182

Harmonia………………………………………..p 131, 143

Hebe……………………………………………….p 10, 112, 120

Hecate…………………………………………….p 23,102,125, 154

Hedone……………………………………………p 170, 184

Hekantonkheires…………………………….p 13

Hekatombaion……………………………….p 65

Helen………………………………………………p 145, 146, 164

Helios……………………………………………..p 21,67,143,154

Hemera…………………………………………..p 45

Hephaestus…………………………………….p 63, 77

Hera………………………………………………..p 17,27,47,84,106

Heraion…………………………………………..p 54

Herakles………………………………………….p 55,89,110,158

Hermaphroditus…………………………….p 142

Hermes	p 63,127,136,162
Herodotus	p 4, 159
Hesiod	p 4, 112,159,164
Hesperides	p 152
Hestia	p 27,47,52,120
Hippokampoi	p 81, 82
Homer	p 92,146,165
Horae	p 33,70,74,75
Hyades	p 152
Hygieia	p 135
Hyperion	p 13, 20, 67
Hypseus	p 139
Hypnos	p 45
Iaso	p 136
Idmon	p 140
Idyia	p 36, 76, 154
Illiad	p 92, 146, 150
Iolchus	p 155, 157
Iphitus	p 158

Iranian……………………………………………………..p 159

Iris…………………………………………………………p 17, 86, 117

Italy……………………………………………………….p 155, 157, 161

Ithaca…………………………………………………….p 146, 157, 161

Jason……………………………………………………..p 55, 110, 154

Judgement of Paris…………………………………p 146, 149

Karmanor……………………………………………….p 58

Karonte………………………………………………….p 185

Khaos…………………………………………………….p 45

Kleio………………………………………………………p 40, 95

Koronis…………………………………………………..p 136

Kos………………………………………………………..p 117

Koios……………………………………………………..p 103

Kratos……………………………………………………p 90, 91

Kronos……………………………………………………p 13

Lachesis…………………………………………………p 70, 71

Lapetus………………………………………………….p 13, 153

Lapiths…………………………………………………..p 140

Latin………………………………………………………p 137, 150

Latinus..p 152, 153

Latium...p 147

Lethe...p 38

Leto..p 23,117,121

Leuke...p 88

Libya..p 141

Ligeia...p 165, 167

Linear B ....p 148

Lipara..p 122

Magpies...p 93

Maia..p 128, 163

Medea..p 55,155,161

Medus...p 159, 160

Megara...p 117

Meliae..p 13, 32, 33

Meligounis...p 143

Melinda..p 17

Melinoe..p 103

Melisseus..p 27

Melpomene	p 40, 103, 165
Meneleus	p 147
Metis	p 36, 77, 107
Minos	p 162
Minotaur	p 162
Mnemosyne	p 32, 38, 40, 92
Moirai	p 15, 33, 70, 72
Mount Dikte	p 25, 31
Mount Ida	p 47
Mount Olympus	p 73, 84, 90, 114
Mount Orthrys	p 5, 27
Mount Pelion	p 85
Mygdon	p 92
Mycenae	p 43, 147
Muses	p 85, 92
Nausinous	p 153
Nausithous	p 153
Neleus	p 156
Nemesis	p 114

Nemesion..p 33

Nephelais..p 36

Nereids..p 80,84,162

Nereus..p 82,103,134

Nerites..p 80

Nestus..p 83

Niobe..p 118

Nyx..p 42,45,70

Oceanids..p 36, 76

Oceanus..p36,58,144

Odomantus..p 92

Odysseus..p17,150,162

Odyssey..p 93,151,166

Oeagrus..p 93

Okeanides..p 36

Olympus..p 115

Olympiads..p 6

Opos..p 123

Oracle..p23,39,84,172

Orestes……………………………………………………p 43, 44

Orion………………………………………………………p 67,122,125

Orpheus…………………………………………………p 93

Ortygia……………………………………………………p 134

Ovid…………………………………………………………p 136

Pallas………………………………………………………p 23,90,111

Paestum…………………………………………………p 166

Pan…………………………………………………………p 122

Panacea…………………………………………………p136,137,139

Pandemos………………………………………………p 64

Pandora…………………………………………………p 168,169,170

Paris…………………………………………………………p 88,146,169

Pasiphae…………………………………………………p 162

Peitho……………………………………………………p 143

Peione……………………………………………………p 127

Peisinoe…………………………………………………p 165, 167

Pelion……………………………………………………p 85

Pelorum…………………………………………………p 165

Peleus……………………………………………………p 84,146,155

Penelope..p 150,152

Pelias..p 55

Peneus...p 140

Perse...p 36,76,155

Perses..p23,103,160

Persephone................................p42,58,103,185

Phoebe......................................p 13,20,32,117

Phobos..p 143

Pianosa..p 64

Pieria..p 40

Pierus..p 93, 94

Pindar...p 4,71,136,140

Pithagorion..p 54

Pjilomelus..p 59

Plato..p 4, 71

Pleiades.................................p 128, 153, 163

Plutus..p 59,75,137,139

Queen..p42,54,104,171

Rhamnous...p 33

Rhea..p26,28,47,52

Rhodos..p 143

Robert Graves..................................p 4

Romans..p26,52,63,165

Salmonius..p 155

Samos..p 54

Scylla..p 150

Scopuli...p 165

Seirenes...p 71

Selene..p 20,71,167

Semele...p 132, 133

Sicily...p 59,65

Sidero...p 155, 156

Siproites...p 122

Sirens...p 93,150, 165

Sirenum..p 165

Sirenuse...p 166

Sparta...p 64, 147

Spindle..p 15, 70

Spring..p 36,73,103

Sphaira..p 15

Steropes..p 13

Styx..p 36,76,90,184

Talos..p 157

Tartarus..p 20, 153

Terpsichore..p 101,165

Tethys..p13,32,47,152

Telphousia..p 42

Thalia..p 40,102, 144

Thaumus...p 86

Thanatos...p 45

Thebes...p 159

Theia..p13,20,32,67

Thelxinoe..p 165, 167

Themis...p13,20,32,70

Themistopoloi..p 33

Theodric..p 17

Theogony..p 160

Thesmophoria..p 59

Theseus..p 159

Thessaly...p 20,60,156

Thetis...p 80,84,146

Thrace..p 93. 140

Tisiphone..p 42

Titans...p 20,47,77

Titanides..p 20,32,86

Titanomachy...p 48,86,153

Tithonos..p 67,169,143

Tityus..p 118

Torchbearer..p 103

Triopas..p 60

Triptolemus..p 58

Triton..p 80

Trojans..p119,146,166

Trojan War...p6,43,88,119

Trophonius..p 39

Troy..p147, 162,166

Tuscan……………………………………………………………p 63, 66

Twice Born…………………………………………………….p 132

Tyro………………………………………………………………p 155, 156

Ulysses…………………………………………………………p 150

Underworld…………………………………………………p 103, 104, 113

Urania………………………………………………………….p 40, 105

Uranus…………………………………………………………p12,20,32,63

Ursa Majore and Minore………………………….p 129

Venus…………………………………………………………..p 63, 64, 66

Vial……………………………………………………………….p 184

Victory…………………………………………………………p 90

Virgil……………………………………………………………..p 147

Virgins………………………………………………………….p 121

Votive……………………………………………………………p 60

Wealth………………………………………………………….p58,73,138,173

Wedding……………………………………………………….p85,146,182

West Wind……………………………………………………p 173

Winged…………………………………………………………p 90, 156

Winter…………………………………………………………..p 104

Wounded..p 88,179,185

Xanthus...p 88

Xenos..p 17

Zagreus..p 103

Zephyros...p 171,174,178

Zeus..p6,15,26,47,58

CPSIA information can be obtained
at www.ICGtesting.com
Printed in the USA
BVHW022247021218
534619BV00011B/62/P